W9-DFD-984

HORSING AROUND

WORKING HORSES

By Jeanne Nagle

Gareth Stevens
Publishing

Please visit our Web site, www.garethstevens.com. For a free color catalog of all our high-quality books, call toll free 1-800-542-2595 or fax 1-877-542-2596.

Library of Congress Cataloging-in-Publication Data

Nagle, Jeanne.
  Working horses / Jeanne Nagle.
      p. cm. – (Horsing around)
  Includes index.
  ISBN 978-1-4339-4644-8 (pbk.)
  ISBN 978-1-4339-4645-5 (6-pack)
  ISBN 978-1-4339-4643-1 (library binding)
  1. Horses—Juvenile literature. 2. Working animals—Juvenile literature. I. Title.
  SF302.N34 2011
  636.1–dc22

                                    2010031273

First Edition

Published in 2011 by
Gareth Stevens Publishing
111 East 14th Street, Suite 349
New York, NY 10003

Copyright © 2011 Gareth Stevens Publishing

Designer: Michael J. Flynn
Editor: Therese Shea

Photo credits: Cover, p. 1, (cover, back cover, p. 1 wooden sign), (pp. 2–5, 7–8, 11–12, 14–15, 17–24 wood background), back cover (wood background), pp. 9, 10 Shutterstock.com; p. 5 Hulton Archive/Getty Images; p. 6 iStockphoto.com; p. 13 William Thomas Cain/ Getty Images; p. 15 Tom Ervin/Getty Images; p. 16 Bertrand Guay/AFP/Getty Images; p. 19 Ken Goff/Time & Life Pictures/Getty Images.

Printed in the United States of America

CPSIA compliance information: Batch #CW11GS: For further information contact Gareth Stevens, New York, New York at 1-800-542-2595.

Contents

Words in the glossary appear in **bold** type the first time they are used in the text.

Horses have lived on Earth for a long time. Some paintings of wild horses found on cave walls are more than 17,000 years old! It wasn't until thousands of years later that horses were **domesticated** so they could help humans.

The first domesticated horses were used for food and milk. Then people rode them. Horses were also used to pull heavy objects such as carts. Farmers depended on horses to pull plows. Many horses still do these kinds of jobs.

This ancient cave painting of a horse is found in Lascaux, France.

THE MANE FACT

Horses were first ridden about 6,000 years ago. This is about 500 years before wheels were first used.

5

Draft horses can pull several times their own weight.

6

Draft Horses

Draft horses are **breeds** that are able to do hard work such as pulling heavy loads. Most draft horses have large, powerful bodies with thick legs. Some work on farms. Others pull **sleighs** in winter or **carriages** in other seasons. In areas where it's hard to drive trucks, draft horses step in. For example, they may drag huge logs out of a forest.

Machines now do most of the work that draft horses once did. Many breeds are disappearing.

THE MANE FACT

Hundred of years ago, draft horses carried knights as they traveled from place to place.

Many breeds of horses work on ranches, which are farms where animals are raised. A ranch horse helps control herds of animals, such as cows. Ranch horses guide the cows from fields to a barn or pen and back again.

Obeying commands from its rider is the most important part of a ranch horse's job. A ranch horse must also have what people call "cow sense." This means the horse can work well with cattle.

Although some ranchers use trucks, many still think horses control herds better.

THE MANE FACT

Some horse shows include events for ranch horses. They do their jobs in front of crowds and judges.

9

Horses are part of police forces around the world. These horses may train for up to 3 years, starting soon after they're born. Police who ride on horseback are called **mounted** police.

Police horses use their large bodies to block people from entering unsafe areas. Sitting on top of a horse allows police officers to see more than they could see from a car or on foot. That's why police horses are used for crowd control.

THE MANE FACT

One of the most famous groups of mounted police is the Royal Canadian Mounties.

11

People who are blind sometimes use animals to guide them. Dogs are used most often. However, **miniature** horses can be guide horses! They're small enough to go most places dogs can go, such as on buses and airplanes.

A horse's eyes are toward the back of its head. This helps the horse see almost all the way around its body without turning its head. Horses can also see well in the dark. These features are helpful in guide animals.

THE MANE FACT

A miniature horse can live to be 50 years old.

Like dogs, miniature horses are trained carefully to be guide horses.

DO NOT TOUCH
Service Animal on Duty

Therapy Horses

Therapy horses help people in several ways. Some people who have problems controlling their bodies ride horses. This activity helps them learn to balance.

Therapy horses are also used to help people who can't talk and work easily with other people. Learning to take care of horses helps people learn to take care of themselves. Feeding and brushing horses also teaches people to be dependable. Horses can also calm people who have deep feelings of anger or sadness.

A gentle horse that obeys people makes a good therapy horse.

"Lunge whips" are long tools used to make noise and lead horses in doing tricks.

16

Some horses **entertain** people. Circus horses learn tricks, such as walking on their back legs with their front legs in the air. They may also jump through hoops and over high bars. Some horses run while circus people stand on their backs!

Many tricks that horses do come from their natural actions. In the wild, horses rear up on their back legs to guard themselves. While running, they may jump over objects such as fallen trees.

THE MANE FACT

Most circus trainers teach their horses using special "clickers" and tasty treats.

Trainers can teach horses to "act" on TV and in movies. Horses that appear on screen must do tricks "on cue," meaning at just the right time. These tricks include standing on their back legs, lying down, nodding, or bowing.

There are often loud noises and bright lights in show business that scare most horses. Acting horses have to be calm and pay attention to their job. Horses that get nervous shouldn't be in show business.

THE MANE FACT

Most acting horses are trained from the day they're born, so they're used to being around people.

18

These horses obey orders even while the actors pretend to fight.

Horses that work during special events are called **ceremonial** horses. Ceremonial horses wear fancy gear. Mounted soldiers often take part in ceremonial parades or other events.

Some horses play sports! **Polo** is a sport in which people ride horses. Players depend on their horses to be quick, make hard turns, and not be afraid of a ball rolling under their hoofs.

THE MANE FACT

The game of polo was played as far back as 525 B.C.!

Horse Breeds at Work

Draft horses	Belgian, Clydesdale, Percheron, shire
Ranch horses	Appaloosa, quarter horse, mustang
Police horses	Morgan, saddlebred, quarter horse
Guide horses	Falabella, miniature horse
Therapy horses	Appaloosa, Morgan, Welsh pony
Circus horses	Andalusian, Arabian, Lipizzaner
Acting horses	any
Carriage horses	Windsor grey, Gelderlander
Polo horses	Arabian, quarter horse, Thoroughbred

Glossary

breed: a group of animals that share features different from others of that kind

carriage: a four-wheeled cart used to carry people

ceremonial: used during special events

domesticate: to train an animal to live with and help humans

entertain: to do things that are interesting to watch or listen to

miniature: a smaller form of something

mounted: riding on a horse

polo: a game played by teams on horseback. Players use long sticks to hit a ball into a goal.

sleigh: an open cart on runners, used for traveling on snow or ice

therapy: a way of dealing with problems that make people's bodies and minds feel better

For More Information

Books:

Apte, Sunita. *Police Horses.* New York, NY: Bearport Publishing, 2007.

Coppendale, Jean. *Horses.* Mankato, MN: QEB Publishing, 2007.

Nichols, Catherine. *Therapy Horses.* New York, NY: Bearport Publishing, 2007.

Web Sites:

Breeds of Livestock: Horses
www.ansi.okstate.edu/breeds/horses/
This Oklahoma State University project lists different horse breeds and their descriptions.

Horses (Equines)
homeschooling.gomilpitas.com/explore/horses.htm
Explore a collection of links and videos on horse breeds, horse care, and horse history.

Index